D1069962

WAR POEMS OF
SIEGFRIED SASSOON

DOVER PUBLICATIONS, INC.
Mineola, New York

EPIGRAPH FROM
Counter-Attack and Other Poems

Dans la trêve désolée de cette matinée, ces hommes
qui avaient été tenaillés par la fatigue, fouettés par
la pluie, bouleversés par toute une nuit de tonnerre,
ces rescapés des volcans et de l'inondation entrevoy-
aient à quel point la guerre, aussi hideuse au moral
qu'au physique, non seulement viole le bon sens, avilit
les grandes idées, commande tous les crimes—mais ils
se rappelaient combien elle avait développé en eux et
autour d'eux tous les mauvais instincts sans en excepter
un seul; la méchanceté jusqu'au sadisme, l'égoïsme
jusqu'à la férocité, le besoin de jouir jusqu'à la folie.

HENRI BARBUSSE.
(*Le Feu.*)

Copyright

Copyright © 2004 by Dover Publications, Inc.
All rights reserved.

Bibliographical Note

This Dover edition, first published in 2004, is a new collection of poems select-
ed from the following volumes: *The Old Huntsman and Other Poems*, as published
in 1918 by E. P. Dutton & Company, New York (originally published in 1917 by
William Heinemann, London); *Counter-Attack and Other Poems*, as published in
1918 by E. P. Dutton & Company, New York; *The War Poems of Siegfried Sassoon*,
as published in 1919 by William Heinemann, London; and *Picture-Show*, as pub-
lished in 1920 by E. P. Dutton & Company, New York. The Introduction by Robert
Nichols first appeared in *Counter-Attack and Other Poems*, cited above.

Library of Congress Cataloging-in-Publication Data

Sassoon, Siegfried, 1886–1967.
    War poems of Siegfried Sassoon.
        p. cm.
    ISBN 0-486-43715-9 (pbk.)
        1. World War, 1914–1918—Poetry. 2 War poetry, English. I. Title.

PR6037.A86A6 2004
821'.912—dc22

                                                                    2004050196

Manufactured in the United States of America
Dover Publications, Inc., 31 East 2nd Street, Mineola, N.Y. 11501

Contents

FROM COUNTER-ATTACK AND OTHER POEMS (1918)

FROM THE WAR POEMS OF SIEGFRIED SASSOON (1919)

FROM PICTURE-SHOW (1920)

Introduction

BY ROBERT NICHOLS[1]

Sassoon the Man

In appearance he is tall, big-boned, loosely built. He is clean-shaven, pale or with a flush; has a heavy jaw, wide mouth with the upper lip slightly protruding and the curve of it very pronounced like that of a shrivelled leaf (as I have noticed is common in many poets). His nose is aquiline, the nostrils being wide and heavily arched. This characteristic and the fullness, depth and heat of his dark eyes give him the air of a sullen falcon. He speaks slowly, enunciating the words as if they pained him, in a voice that has something of the troubled thickness apparent in the voices of those who emerge from a deep grief. As he speaks, his large hands, roughened by trench toil and by riding, wander aimlessly until some emotion grips him when the knuckles harden and he clutches at his knees or at the edge of the table. And all the while he will be breathing hard like a man who has swum a distance. When he reads his poems he chants and one would think that he communed with himself save that, at the pauses, he shoots a powerful glance at the listener. Between the poems he is still but moves his lips. . . . He likes best to speak of hunting (he will shout of it!), of open air mornings when the gorse alone flames brighter than the sky, of country quiet, of his mother,[2] of poetry—usually Shelley, Masefield and Thomas Hardy—

---

[1]Robert Nichols (1893–1944) was, like his good friend Siegfried Sassoon (1886–1967), both a poet and a soldier who served in the First World War. His Introduction originally appeared in Sassoon's *Counter-Attack and Other Poems* (1918), one of the volumes used to compile the current work (see Contents, page iv). [ED.]

[2]His father was a well-to-do country gentleman of Anglo-Jewish stock, his mother an English woman, a Miss Thornycroft, sister of the sculptor of that name. [R.N.]

and last and chiefly—but always with a rapid, tumbling enunci-
ation and a much-irked desperate air filled with pain—of sol-
diers. For the incubus of war is on him so that his days are shot
with anguish and his nights with horror.

He is twenty-eight years old; was educated at Marlborough
and Christchurch, Oxford; was a master of fox-hounds and is a
captain in the Royal Welsh Fusiliers. Thrice he has fought in
France and once in Palestine. Behind his name are set the let-
ters M.C. since he has won the Military Cross for an act of val-
our which went near to securing him a higher honour.

Sassoon the Poet

The poetry of Siegfried Sassoon divides itself into two rough
classes—the idyllic and the satiric. War has defiled one to pro-
duce the other. At heart Siegfried Sassoon is an idealist.

Before the war he had hardly published a line. He spent his
summers in the company of books, at the piano, on expeditions,
and in playing tennis. During winter he hunted. Hunting was a
greater passion with him than poetry. Much of his poetry cele-
brated the loveliness of the field as seen by the huntsman in the
early morning light. But few probably guessed that the youth
known to excel in field sports excelled also in poetry. For, in its
way, this early poetry does excel. It was characteristic of him that
nearly every little book he then wrote was privately printed.
Poetry was for him just something for private and particular
enjoyment—like a ride alone before breakfast. Among these pri-
vately printed books are *Twelve Sonnets* (1911), *Melodies, An Ode
for Music, Hyacinth* (all 1912). The names are significant. He was
occupied with natural beauty and with music. In 1913 he pub-
lishes in a limited and obscure edition *Apollo in Doelyrium,*
wherein it seems that he is beginning to find a certain want of
body and basis in his poems made of beautiful words about beau-
tiful objects. Later in the same year, with Masefield's *Everlasting
Mercy* (1911), *Widow in the Bye Sheet* (1912) and *Daffodil Fields*
(1913) before him, he starts to write a parody of these uncouth
intrusions of the sorrows of obscure persons into his paradise but
half way through the poem adopts the Masefield manner in

earnest[3] and finishes by unsuccessfully endeavouring to rival his master. In 1914 the War breaks out. Home on leave in 1915 he privately prints *Discoveries*, a little book which contains some of the loveliest of his "paradise" poems. In 1916 the change has come. He can hardly believe it himself. *Morning Glory* (privately printed) includes four war poems. He has not definitely turned to his later style but he hovers on the brink. The war is beginning to pain him. The poems "To Victory" and "The Dragon and the Undying" show him turning toward his paradise to see if its beauty can save him . . . The year 1917 witnesses the publication of *The Old Huntsman*.[4] This book secured instantaneous success. Siegfried Sassoon, on its publication, became one of the leading young poets of England. The book begins with the long monologue of a retired huntsman, a piece of remarkable characterisation. It continues with all the best of the "paradise" poems, including the loveliest in *Discoveries* and *Morning Glory*. There are also the "bridge" poems between his old manner and his new such as the "To Victory" mentioned above. But interspersed among the paradise poems are the first poems in his final war style. He tells the story of the change in a characteristic manner— "Conscripts."[5] For like nearly every one of the young English poets, he is to some extent a humourist. His humour is not, however, even through *The Old Huntsman* all of such a wise and gentle tenor. He breaks out into lively bitterness in such poems as "'They,'" "The Tombstone Maker" and "'Blighters.'"

This book (in consequence almost wholly of these bitter poems) enjoyed a remarkable success with the soldiers fighting in France. One met it everywhere. "Hello, you know Siegfried Sassoon then, do you? Well, tell him from me that the more he lays it on thick to those who don't realize the war the better. That's the stuff we want. We're fed up with the old men's death-or-glory stunt." In 1918 appeared *Countermans' Attack*[6] [sic]:

---

[3]I had this from his own mouth. [R.N.]
[4]See pages 1 to 46 for poems from this collection. [ED.]
[5]The full text of the poem "Conscripts" appeared between this paragraph and the next in the original version of this Introduction, but is omitted above since it is included in its entirety on pages 30 to 31. [ED.]
[6]*Counter-Attack and Other Poems*, see pages 47 to 91. [ED.]

here there is hardly a trace of the "paradise" feeling. You can't even think of paradise when you're in hell. For Sassoon was now well along the way of thorns. How many lives had he not seen spilled apparently to no purpose? Did not the fact of war arch him in like a dirty blood-red sky? He breaks out, almost like a mad man, into imprecations, into vehement tirades, into sarcasms, ironies, the hellish laughters that arise from a heart that is not broken once for all but that is newly broken every day while the Monster that devours the lives of the young continues its ravages. Take, for instance, the magnificent "To Any Dead Officer," written just before America entered the war. Many reading this poem would think Great Britain was going to cease fighting. But nothing of the sort. One must always remember that bitter as these imprecations are against those who mismanaged certain episodes in the war, the ultimate foe is not they but the German Junkers who planned this war for forty years, who have given the lovely earth over to hideous defilement and the youths of all nations to carnage . . .

Sometimes in this book Sassoon fails to express himself properly. This fact is, I think, a tribute to his sincerity. For his earlier work very clearly displays his technical proficiency. But here what can he do? Indignation chokes and strangles him. He claws often enough at unsatisfactory words, dislocates his sentences, tumbles out his images as if he would pulp the makers of war beneath them. Very rarely does he attain to the poignant simplicity of "The Hawthorn Tree" or the detached irony of "Does it Matter?"

Can he then see nothing else in war? I remember him once turning to me and saying suddenly apropos of certain *exalté* poems in my *Ardours and Endurances* [1917]: "Yes, I see all that and I agree with you, Robert. War has made me. I think I am a man now as well as a poet. You have said the things well enough. Now let us nevermore say another word of whatever little may be good in war for the individual who has a heart to be steeled."

I remember I nodded, for further acquaintance with war inclines me to his opinion.

"Let no one ever," he continued, "from henceforth say a word in any way countenancing war. It is dangerous even to speak of how here and there the individual may gain some hardship of soul by it. For war is hell and those who institute it are criminals. Were there anything to say for it, it should not be said for its spiritual disasters far outweigh any of its advantages."

For myself this is the truth. War doesn't ennoble: it degrades. The words of Barbusse placed at the beginning of this book[7] should be engraved over the doors of every war office of every State in the world.

While war is a possibility man is little better than a savage and civilisation the mere moments of rest between a succession of nightmares. It is to help to end this horror that Siegfried Sassoon and the many others who feel like him have continued to fight as after the publication of this book he fought in Palestine and in France.

You civilized persons who read this book not only as a poet but as a soldier I beg of you not to turn from it. Read it again and again till its words become part of your consciousness. It was written by a man for mankind's sake, that might once more become "that which is humane" not an empty phrase, that the words of Blake might blossom to a new meaning—

> *Thou art a man, God is no more,*
> *Thine own humanity learn to adore.*

New York City,   ROBERT NICHOLS
  Nov. 20th–23rd.

---

[7]See page ii of this edition for the quotation from Barbusse that appeared as the epigraph for *Counter-Attack and Other Poems*. [ED.]

Absolution

THE anguish of the earth absolves our eyes
Till beauty shines in all that we can see.
War is our scourge; yet war has made us wise,
And, fighting for our freedom, we are free.

Horror of wounds and anger at the foe,
And loss of things desired; all these must pass.
We are the happy legion, for we know
Time's but a golden wind that shakes the grass.

There was an hour when we were loth to part
From life we longed to share no less than others.
Now, having claimed this heritage of heart,
What need we more, my comrades and my brothers?

Brothers

GIVE me your hand, my brother, search my face;
Look in these eyes lest I should think of shame.
For we have made an end of all things base;
We are returning by the road we came.

Your lot is with the ghosts of soldiers dead,
And I am in the field where men must fight.
But in the gloom I see your laurell'd head
And through your victory I shall win the light.

The Dragon and the Undying

ALL night the flares go up; the Dragon sings
And beats upon the dark with furious wings;
And, stung to rage by his own darting fires,
Reaches with grappling coils from town to town;
He lusts to break the loveliness of spires,
And hurls their martyred music toppling down.

Yet, though the slain are homeless as the breeze,
Vocal are they, like storm-bewilder'd seas.
Their faces are the fair, unshrouded night,
And planets are their eyes, their ageless dreams.
Tenderly stooping earthward from their height,
They wander in the dusk with chanting streams;
And they are dawn-lit trees, with arms up-flung,
To hail the burning heavens they left unsung.

France

SHE triumphs, in the vivid green
Where sun and quivering foliage meet;
And in each soldier's heart serene;
When death stood near them they have seen
The radiant forests where her feet
Move on a breeze of silver sheen.

And they are fortunate, who fight
For gleaming landscapes swept and shafted
And crowned by cloud pavilions white;
Hearing such harmonies as might
Only from Heaven be downward wafted—
Voices of victory and delight.

To Victory

[To Edmund Gosse]

RETURN to greet me, colours that were my joy,
Not in the woeful crimson of men slain,
But shining as a garden; come with the streaming
Banners of dawn and sundown after rain.

I want to fill my gaze with blue and silver,
Radiance through living roses, spires of green
Rising in young-limbed copse and lovely wood
Where the hueless wind passes and cries unseen.

I am not sad; only I long for lustre,—
Tired of the greys and browns and the leafless ash.
I would have hours that move like a glitter of dancers
Far from the angry guns that boom and flash.

Return, musical, gay with blossom and fleetness,
Days when my sight shall be clear and my heart rejoice;
Come from the sea with breadth of approaching brightness,
When the blithe wind laughs on the hills with uplifted voice.

When I'm among a Blaze of Lights . . .

WHEN I'm among a blaze of lights,
With tawdry music and cigars
And women dawdling through delights,
And officers at cocktail bars,—
Sometimes I think of garden nights
And elm trees nodding at the stars.

I dream of a small firelit room
With yellow candles burning straight,
And glowing pictures in the gloom,
And kindly books that hold me late.
Of things like these I love to think
When I can never be alone:
Then someone says, "Another drink?"—
And turns my living heart to stone.

Golgotha

THROUGH darkness curves a spume of falling flares
That flood the field with shallow, blanching light.
    The huddled sentry stares
    On gloom at war with white,
    And white receding slow, submerged in gloom.
    Guns into mimic thunder burst and boom,
    And mirthless laughter rakes the whistling night.
The sentry keeps his watch where no one stirs
But the brown rats, the nimble scavengers.

A Mystic as Soldier

I LIVED my days apart,
Dreaming fair songs for God,
By the glory in my heart
Covered and crowned and shod.

Now God is in the strife,
And I must seek Him there,
Where death outnumbers life,
And fury smites the air.

I walk the secret way
With anger in my brain.
O music through my clay,
When will you sound again?

The Kiss

To these I turn, in these I trust;
Brother Lead and Sister Steel.
To his blind power I make appeal;
I guard her beauty clean from rust.

He spins and burns and loves the air,
And splits a skull to win my praise;
But up the nobly marching days
She glitters naked, cold and fair.

Sweet Sister, grant your soldier this:
That in good fury he may feel
The body where he sets his heel
Quail from your downward darting kiss.

The Redeemer

DARKNESS: the rain sluiced down; the mire was deep;
It was past twelve on a mid-winter night,
When peaceful folk in beds lay snug asleep:
There, with much work to do before the light,
We lugged our clay-sucked boots as best we might
Along the trench; sometimes a bullet sang,
And droning shells burst with a hollow bang;
We were soaked, chilled and wretched, every one.
Darkness: the distant wink of a huge gun.

I turned in the black ditch, loathing the storm;
A rocket fizzed and burned with blanching flare,
And lit the face of what had been a form
Floundering in mirk. He stood before me there;
I say that he was Christ; stiff in the glare,
And leaning forward from his burdening task,
Both arms supporting it; his eyes on mine
Stared from the woeful head that seemed a mask
Of mortal pain in Hell's unholy shine.

No thorny crown, only a woollen cap
He wore—an English soldier, white and strong,
Who loved his time like any simple chap,
Good days of work and sport and homely song;
Now he has learned that nights are very long,
And dawn a watching of the windowed sky.
But to the end, unjudging, he'll endure
Horror and pain, not uncontent to die
That Lancaster on Lune may stand secure.

He faced me, reeling in his weariness,
Shouldering his load of planks, so hard to bear.
I say that he was Christ, who wrought to bless
All groping things with freedom bright as air,
And with His mercy washed and made them fair.
Then the flame sank, and all grew black as pitch,
While we began to struggle along the ditch;
And someone flung his burden in the muck,
Mumbling: "O Christ Almighty, now I'm stuck!"

A Subaltern

HE turned to me with his kind, sleepy gaze
And fresh face slowly brightening to the grin
That sets my memory back to summer days
With twenty runs to make, and last man in.
He told me he'd been having a bloody time
In trenches, crouching for the "crumps"* to burst,
While squeaking rats scampered across the slime
And the grey palsied weather did its worst.
But as he stamped and shivered in the rain,
My stale philosophies had served him well;
Dreaming about his girl had sent his brain
Blanker than ever—she'd no place in Hell. . . .
"Good God!" he laughed, and calmly filled his pipe,
Wondering "why he always talked such tripe."

---

*A crump is a shell or bomb. [ED.]

"In the Pink"

So Davies wrote: "This leaves me in the pink."
Then scrawled his name: "Your loving sweetheart, Willie."
With crosses for a hug. He'd had a drink
Of rum and tea; and, though the barn was chilly,
For once his blood ran warm; he had pay to spend.
Winter was passing; soon the year would mend.

He couldn't sleep that night. Stiff in the dark
He groaned and thought of Sundays at the farm,
When he'd go out as cheerful as a lark
In his best suit to wander arm-in-arm
With brown-eyed Gwen, and whisper in her ear
The simple, silly things she liked to hear.

And then he thought: to-morrow night we trudge
Up to the trenches, and my boots are rotten.
Five miles of stodgy clay and freezing sludge,
And everything but wretchedness forgotten.
To-night he's in the pink; but soon he'll die.
And still the war goes on; *he* don't know why.

A Working Party

THREE hours ago he blundered up the trench,
Sliding and poising, groping with his boots;
Sometimes he tripped and lurched against the walls
With hands that pawed the sodden bags of chalk.
He couldn't see the man who walked in front;
Only he heard the drum and rattle of feet
Stepping along the trench-boards,—often splashing
Wretchedly where the sludge was ankle-deep.

Voices would grunt, "Keep to your right,—make way!"
When squeezing past the men from the front-line:
White faces peered, puffing a point of red;
Candles and braziers glinted through the chinks
And curtain-flaps of dug-outs; then the gloom
Swallowed his sense of sight; he stooped and swore
Because a sagging wire had caught his neck.

A flare went up; the shining whiteness spread
And flickered upward, showing nimble rats,
And mounds of glimmering sand-bags, bleached with rain;
Then the slow, silver moment died in dark.
The wind came posting by with chilly gusts
And buffeting at corners, piping thin
And dreary through the crannies; rifle-shots
Would split and crack and sing along the night,
And shells came calmly through the drizzling air
To burst with hollow bang below the hill.

Three hours ago he stumbled up the trench;
Now he will never walk that road again:

He must be carried back, a jolting lump
Beyond all need of tenderness and care;
A nine-stone corpse with nothing more to do.

He was a young man with a meagre wife
And two pale children in a Midland town;
He showed the photograph to all his mates;
And they considered him a decent chap
Who did his work and hadn't much to say,
And always laughed at other people's jokes
Because he hadn't any of his own.

That night, when he was busy at his job
Of piling bags along the parapet,
He thought how slow time went, stamping his feet,
And blowing on his fingers, pinched with cold.
He thought of getting back by half-past twelve,
And tot of rum to send him warm to sleep
In draughty dug-out frowsty with the fumes
Of coke, and full of snoring, weary men.

He pushed another bag along the top,
Craning his body outward; then a flare
Gave one white glimpse of No Man's Land and wire;
And as he dropped his head the instant split
His startled life with lead, and all went out.

A Whispered Tale

[To J.D.]

I'D heard fool-heroes brag of where they'd been,
With stories of the glories that they'd seen,
Till there was nothing left for shame to screen.

But you, good, simple soldier, seasoned well
In woods and posts and crater-lines of hell,
Who dodge remembered "crumps" with wry grimace,—
Cold hours of torment in your queer, kind face,
Smashed bodies in your strained, unhappy eyes,
And both your brothers killed to make you wise;
You had no empty babble; what you said
Was like a whisper from the maimed and dead.
But Memory brought the voice I knew, whose note
Was smothered when they shot you in the throat;
And still you whisper of the war, and find
Sour jokes for all those horrors left behind.

"Blighters"

THE House is crammed: tier beyond tier they grin
And cackle at the Show, while prancing ranks
Of harlots shrill the chorus, drunk with din;
"We're sure the Kaiser loves the dear old Tanks!"

I'd like to see a Tank come down the stalls,
Lurching to ragtime tunes, or "Home, sweet Home,"—
And there'd be no more jokes in Music-halls
To mock the riddled corpses round Bapaume.

At Carnoy

Down in the hollow there's the whole Brigade
Camped in four groups: through twilight falling slow
I hear a sound of mouth-organs, ill-played,
And murmur of voices, gruff, confused, and low.
Crouched among thistle-tufts I've watched the glow
Of a blurred orange sunset flare and fade;
And I'm content. To-morrow we must go
To take some cursèd Wood . . . O world God made!

July 3rd, 1916.

To His Dead Body

WHEN roaring gloom surged inward and you cried,
Groping for friendly hands, and clutched, and died,
Like racing smoke, swift from your lolling head
Phantoms of thoughts and memory thinned and fled.

Yet, though my dreams that throng the darkened stair
Can bring me no report of how you fare,
Safe quit of wars, I speed you on your way
Up lonely, glimmering fields to find new day,
Slow-rising, saintless, confident and kind—
Dear, red-faced father God who lit your mind.

Two Hundred Years After

TRUDGING by Corbie Ridge one winter's night,
(Unless old, hearsay memories tricked his sight),
Along the pallid edge of the quiet sky
He watched a nosing lorry grinding on,
And straggling files of men; when these were gone,
A double limber and six mules went by,
Hauling the rations up through ruts and mud
To trench-lines digged two hundred years ago.
Then darkness hid them with a rainy scud,
And soon he saw the village lights below.

But when he'd told his tale, an old man said
That *he'd* seen soldiers pass along that hill;
"Poor, silent things, they were the English dead
"Who came to fight in France and got their fill."

"They"

THE Bishop tells us: "When the boys come back
"They will not be the same; for they'll have fought
"In a just cause: they lead the last attack
"On Anti-Christ; their comrade's blood has bought
"New right to breed an honourable race.
"They have challenged Death and dared him face to face."

"We're none of us the same!" the boys reply.
"For George lost both his legs; and Bill's stone blind;
"Poor Jim's shot through the lungs and like to die;
"And Bert's gone syphilitic: you'll not find
"A chap who's served that hasn't found *some* change."
And the Bishop said: "The ways of God are strange!"

Stand-to: Good Friday Morning

I'D been on duty from two till four.
I went and stared at the dug-out door.
Down in the frowst I heard them snore.
"Stand to!" Somebody grunted and swore.
   Dawn was misty; the skies were still;
   Larks were singing, discordant, shrill;
   They seemed happy; but *I* felt ill.
Deep in water I splashed my way
Up the trench to our bogged front line.
Rain had fallen the whole damned night.
O Jesus, send me a wound to-day,
And I'll believe in Your bread and wine,
And get my bloody old sins washed white!

                  •

The One-Legged Man

PROPPED on a stick he viewed the August weald;
Squat orchard trees and oasts with painted cowls;
A homely, tangled hedge, a corn-stooked field,
With sound of barking dogs and farmyard fowls.

And he'd come home again to find it more
Desirable than ever it was before.
How right it seemed that he should reach the span
Of comfortable years allowed to man!
Splendid to eat and sleep and choose a wife,
Safe with his wound, a citizen of life.
He hobbled blithely through the garden gate,
And thought: "Thank God they had to amputate!"

Enemies

HE stood alone in some queer sunless place
Where Armageddon ends; perhaps he longed
For days he might have lived; but his young face
Gazed forth untroubled: and suddenly there thronged
Round him the hulking Germans that I shot
When for his death my brooding rage was hot.

He stared at them, half-wondering; and then
They told him how I'd killed them for his sake,—
Those patient, stupid, sullen ghosts of men:
And still there seemed no answer he could make.
At last he turned and smiled, and all was well
Because his face could lead them out of hell.

The Tombstone-Maker

HE primmed his loose red mouth, and leaned his head
Against a sorrowing angel's breast, and said:
"You'd think so much bereavement would have made
"Unusual big demands upon my trade.
"The War comes cruel hard on some poor folk—
"Unless the fighting stops I'll soon be broke."

He eyed the Cemetery across the road—
"There's scores of bodies out abroad, this while,
"That should be here by rights; they little know'd
"How they'd get buried in such wretched style."

I told him, with a sympathetic grin,
That Germans boil dead soldiers down for fat;
And he was horrified. "What shameful sin!
"O sir, that Christian men should come to that!"

Arms and the Man

YOUNG Crœsus went to pay his call
On Colonel Sawbones, Caxton Hall:
And, though his wound was healed and mended,
He hoped he'd get his leave extended.

The waiting-room was dark and bare.
He eyed a neat-framed notice there
Above the fireplace hung to show
Disabled heroes where to go
For arms and legs; with scale of price,
And words of dignified advice
How officers could get them free.

Elbow or shoulder, hip or knee,—
Two arms, two legs, though all were lost,
They'd be restored him free of cost.

Then a Girl-Guide looked in to say,
"Will Captain Crœsus come this way?"

Died of Wounds

HIS wet, white face and miserable eyes
Brought nurses to him more than groans and sighs:
But hoarse and low and rapid rose and fell
His troubled voice: he did the business well.

The ward grew dark; but he was still complaining,
And calling out for "Dickie." "Curse the Wood!
"It's time to go; O Christ, and what's the good?—
"We'll never take it; and it's always raining."

I wondered where he'd been; then heard him shout,
"They snipe like hell! O Dickie, don't go out" . . .
I fell asleep . . . next morning he was dead;
And some Slight Wound lay smiling on his bed.

The Hero

"JACK fell as he'd have wished," the Mother said,
And folded up the letter that she'd read.
"The Colonel writes so nicely." Something broke
In the tired voice that quavered to a choke.
She half looked up. "We mothers are so proud
"Of our dead soldiers." Then her face was bowed.

Quietly the Brother Officer went out.
He'd told the poor old dear some gallant lies
That she would nourish all her days, no doubt.
For while he coughed and mumbled, her weak eyes
Had shone with gentle triumph, brimmed with joy,
Because he'd been so brave, her glorious boy.

He thought how "Jack," cold-footed, useless swine,
Had panicked down the trench that night the mine
Went up at Wicked Corner; how he'd tried
To get sent home; and how, at last, he died,
Blown to small bits. And no one seemed to care
Except that lonely woman with white hair.

Stretcher Case

[To Edward Marsh]

He woke: the clank and racket of the train
Kept time with angry throbbings in his brain.
Then for a while he lapsed and drowsed again.

At last he lifted his bewildered eyes
And blinked, and rolled them sidelong; hills and skies,
Heavily wooded, hot with August haze,
And, slipping backward, golden for his gaze,
Acres of harvest.

           Feebly now he drags
Exhausted ego back from glooms and quags
And blasting tumult, terror, hurtling glare,
To calm and brightness, havens of sweet air.
He sighed, confused; then drew a cautious breath;
This level journeying was no ride through death.
"If I were dead," he mused, "there'd be no thinking—
"Only some plunging underworld of sinking,
"And hueless, shifting welter where I'd drown."

Then he remembered that his name was Brown.

But was he back in Blighty? Slow he turned,
Till in his heart thanksgiving leapt and burned.
There shone the blue serene, the prosperous land,
Trees, cows and hedges; skipping these, he scanned
Large, friendly names that change not with the year,
Lung Tonic, Mustard, Liver Pills and Beer.

Conscripts

"FALL in, that awkward squad, and strike no more
"Attractive attitudes! Dress by the right!
"The luminous rich colours that you wore
"Have changed to hueless khaki in the night.
"Magic? What's magic got to do with you?
"There's no such thing! Blood's red and skies are blue."

They gasped and sweated, marching up and down.
I drilled them till they cursed my raucous shout.
Love chucked his lute away and dropped his crown.
Rhyme got sore heels and wanted to fall out.
"Left, right! Press on your butts!" They looked at me
Reproachful; how I longed to set them free!

I gave them lectures on Defence, Attack;
They fidgeted and shuffled, yawned and sighed,
And boggled at my questions. Joy was slack,
And Wisdom gnawed his fingers, gloomy-eyed.
Young Fancy—how I loved him all the while—
Stared at his note-book with a rueful smile.

Their training done, I shipped them all to France.
Where most of those I'd loved too well got killed.
Rapture and pale Enchantment and Romance,
And many a sickly, slender lord who'd filled
My soul long since with lutanies of sin,
Went home, because they couldn't stand the din.

But the kind, common ones that I despised,
(Hardly a man of them I'd count as friend),
What stubborn-hearted virtues they disguised!
They stood and played the hero to the end,
Won gold and silver medals bright with bars,
And marched resplendent home with crowns and stars.

The Road

THE road is thronged with women; soldiers pass
And halt, but never see them; yet they're here—
A patient crowd along the sodden grass,
Silent, worn out with waiting, sick with fear.
The road goes crawling up a long hillside,
All ruts and stones and sludge, and the emptied dregs
Of battle thrown in heaps. Here where they died
Are stretched big-bellied horses with stiff legs;
And dead men, bloody-fingered from the fight,
Stare up at caverned darkness winking white.

You in the bomb-scorched kilt, poor sprawling Jock,
You tottered here and fell, and stumbled on,
Half dazed for want of sleep. No dream could mock
Your reeling brain with comforts lost and gone.
You did not feel her arms about your knees,
Her blind caress, her lips upon your head:
Too tired for thoughts of home and love and ease,
The road would serve you well enough for bed.

Secret Music

I KEEP such music in my brain
No din this side of death can quell,—
Glory exulting over pain,
And beauty, garlanded in hell.

My dreaming spirit will not heed
The roar of guns that would destroy
My life that on the gloom can read
Proud-surging melodies of joy.

To the world's end I went, and found
Death in his carnival of glare;
But in my anguish I was crowned,
And music dawned above despair.

Haunted

EVENING was in the wood, louring with storm.
A time of drought had sucked the weedy pool
And baked the channels; birds had done with song.
Thirst was a dream of fountains in the moon,
Or willow-music blown across the water
Leisurely sliding on by weir and mill.

Uneasy was the man who wandered, brooding,
His face a little whiter than the dusk.
A drone of sultry wings flicker'd in his head.

The end of sunset burning thro' the boughs
Died in a smear of red; exhausted hours
Cumber'd, and ugly sorrows hemmed him in.

He thought: "Somewhere there's thunder," as he strove
To shake off dread; he dared not look behind him,
But stood, the sweat of horror on his face.

He blundered down a path, trampling on thistles,
In sudden race to leave the ghostly trees.
And: "Soon I'll be in open fields," he thought,
And half remembered starlight on the meadows,
Scent of mown grass and voices of tired men,
Fading along the field-paths; home and sleep
And cool-swept upland spaces, whispering leaves,
And far off the long churring night-jar's note.

But something in the wood, trying to daunt him,
Led him confused in circles through the brake.

He was forgetting his old wretched folly,
And freedom was his need; his throat was choking;
Barbed brambles gripped and clawed him round his legs,
And he floundered over snags and hidden stumps.
Mumbling: "I will get out! I must get out!"
Butting and thrusting up the baffling gloom,
Pausing to listen in a space 'twixt thorns,
He peers around with boding, frantic eyes.
An evil creature in the twilight looping,
Flapped blindly in his face. Beating it off,
He screeched in terror, and straightway something clambered
Heavily from an oak, and dropped, bent double,
To shamble at him zigzag, squat and bestial.

Headlong he charges down the wood, and falls
With roaring brain—agony—the snap't spark—
And blots of green and purple in his eyes.
Then the slow fingers groping on his neck,
And at his heart the strangling clasp of death.

Before the Battle

MUSIC of whispering trees
Hushed by a broad-winged breeze
Where shaken water gleams;
And evening radiance falling
With reedy bird-notes calling.
O bear me safe through dark, you low-voiced streams.

I have no need to pray
That fear may pass away;
I scorn the growl and rumble of the fight
That summons me from cool
Silence of marsh and pool,
And yellow lilies islanded in light.
O river of stars and shadows, lead me through the night.

June 25th, 1916.

The Death-Bed

HE drowsed and was aware of silence heaped
Round him, unshaken as the steadfast walls;
Aqueous like floating rays of amber light,
Soaring and quivering in the wings of sleep,—
Silence and safety; and his mortal shore
Lipped by the inward, moonless waves of death.

Someone was holding water to his mouth.
He swallowed, unresisting; moaned and dropped
Through crimson gloom to darkness; and forgot
The opiate throb and ache that was his wound.
Water—calm, sliding green above the weir;
Water—a sky-lit alley for his boat,
Bird-voiced, and bordered with reflected flowers
And shaken hues of summer: drifting down,
He dipped contented oars, and sighed, and slept.

Night, with a gust of wind, was in the ward,
Blowing the curtain to a glimmering curve.
Night. He was blind; he could not see the stars
Glinting among the wraiths of wandering cloud;
Queer blots of colour, purple, scarlet, green,
Flickered and faded in his drowning eyes.

Rain; he could hear it rustling through the dark;
Fragrance and passionless music woven as one;
Warm rain on drooping roses; pattering showers
That soak the woods; not the harsh rain that sweeps
Behind the thunder, but a trickling peace
Gently and slowly washing life away.

He stirred, shifting his body; then the pain
Leaped like a prowling beast, and gripped and tore
His groping dreams with grinding claws and fangs.
But someone was beside him; soon he lay
Shuddering because that evil thing had passed.
And death, who'd stepped toward him, paused and stared.

Light many lamps and gather round his bed.
Lend him your eyes, warm blood, and will to live.
Speak to him; rouse him; you may save him yet.
He's young; he hated war; how should he die
When cruel old campaigners win safe through?

But Death replied: "I choose him." So he went,
And there was silence in the summer night;
Silence and safety; and the veils of sleep.
Then, far away, the thudding of the guns.

The Last Meeting

BECAUSE the night was falling warm and still
Upon a golden day at April's end,
I thought; I will go up the hill once more
To find the face of him that I have lost,
And speak with him before his ghost has flown
Far from the earth that might not keep him long.

So down the road I went, pausing to see
How slow the dusk drew on, and how the folk
Loitered about their doorways, well-content
With the fine weather and the waxing year.
The miller's house, that glimmered with grey walls,
Turned me aside; and for a while I leaned
Along the tottering rail beside the bridge
To watch the dripping mill-wheel green with damp.
The miller peered at me with shadowed eyes
And pallid face: I could not hear his voice
For the insistent water. He was old:
His days went round with the unhurrying wheel.

Moving along the street, each side I saw
The humble, kindly folk in lamp-lit rooms;
Children at table; simple, homely wives;
Strong, grizzled men; and soldiers back from war,
Scaring the gaping elders with loud talk.

Soon all the jumbled roofs were down the hill,
And I was turning up the grassy lane

39

That goes to the big, empty house that stands
Above the town, half-hid by towering trees.
I looked below and saw the glinting lights:
I heard the treble cries of bustling life,
And mirth, and scolding; and the grind of wheels.
An engine whistled, piercing-shrill, and called
High echoes from the sombre slopes afar;
Then a long line of trucks began to move.
It was quite still; the columned chestnuts stood
Dark in their noble canopies of leaves.
I thought: "A little longer I'll delay,
"And then he'll be more glad to hear my feet,
"And with low laughter ask me why I'm late.
"The place will be too dim to show his eyes,
"But he will loom above me like a tree,
"With lifted arms and body tall and strong."

There stood the empty house; a ghostly hulk
Becalmed and huge, massed in the mantling dark,
As builders left it when quick-shattering war
Leapt upon France and called her men to fight.
Lightly along the terraces I trod,
Crunching the rubble till I found the door
That gaped in twilight, framing inward gloom.
An owl flew out from under the high eaves
To vanish secretly among the firs,
Where lofty boughs netted the gleam of stars.
I stumbled in; the dusty floors were strewn
With cumbering piles of planks and props and beams;
Tall windows gapped the walls; the place was free
To every searching gust and jousting gale;
But now they slept; I was afraid to speak,
And heavily the shadows crowded in.

I called him, once; then listened: nothing moved:
Only my thumping heart beat out the time.
Whispering his name, I groped from room to room.

Quite empty was that house; it could not hold
His human ghost, remembered in the love
That strove in vain to be companioned still.

II.

Blindly I sought the woods that I had known
So beautiful with morning when I came
Amazed with spring that wove the hazel copse
With misty raiment of awakening green.
I found a holy dimness, and the peace
Of sanctuary, austerely built of trees,
And wonder stooping from the tranquil sky.

Ah! but there was no need to call his name.
He was beside me now, as swift as light.
I knew him crushed to earth in scentless flowers,
And lifted in the rapture of dark pines.
"For now," he said, "my spirit has more eyes
"Than heaven has stars; and they are lit by love.
My body is the magic of the world,
And dawn and sunset flame with my spilt blood.
My breath is the great wind, and I am filled
With molten power and surge of the bright waves
That chant my doom along the ocean's edge.

"Look in the faces of the flowers and find
The innocence that shrives me; stoop to the stream
That you may share the wisdom of my peace.
For talking water travels undismayed.
The luminous willows lean to it with tales
Of the young earth; and swallows dip their wings
Where showering hawthorn strews the lanes of light.

"I can remember summer in one thought
Of wind-swept green, and deeps of melting blue,
And scent of limes in bloom; and I can hear

Distinct the early mower in the grass,
Whetting his blade along some morn of June.

"For I was born to the round world's delight,
And knowledge of enfolding motherhood,
Whose tenderness, that shines through constant toil,
Gathers the naked children to her knees.
In death I can remember how she came
To kiss me while I slept; still I can share
The glee of childhood; and the fleeting gloom
When all my flowers were washed with rain of tears.

"I triumph in the choruses of birds,
Bursting like April buds in gyres of song,
My meditations are the blaze of noon
On silent woods where glory burns the leaves.
I have shared breathless vigils; I have slaked
The thirst of my desires in bounteous rain
Pouring and splashing downward through the dark.
Loud storm has roused me with its winking glare,
And voice of doom that crackles overhead.
I have been tired and watchful, craving rest,
Till the slow-footed hours have touched my brows
And laid me on the breast of sundering sleep."

III.

I know that he is lost among the stars,
And may return no more but in their light.
Though his hushed voice may call me in the stir
Of whispering trees I shall not understand.
Men may not speak with stillness; and the joy
Of brooks that leap and tumble down green hills
Is faster than their feet; and all their songs
Can win no meaning from the talk of birds.

My heart is fooled with fancies, being wise;
For fancy is the gleaming of wet flowers

When the hid sun looks forth with golden stare.
Thus, when I find new loveliness to praise,
And things long-known shine out in sudden grace,
Then will I think: "He moves before me now."
So he will never come but in delight;
And, as it was in life, his name shall be
Wonder awaking in a summer dawn,
And youth, that dying, touched my lips to song.

A Letter Home

[To Robert Graves]

I.

Here I'm sitting in the gloom
Of my quiet attic room.
France goes rolling all around,
Fledged with forest May has crowned.
And I puff my pipe, calm-hearted,
Thinking how the fighting started,
Wondering when we'll ever end it,
Back to Hell with Kaiser send it,
Gag the noise, pack up and go,
Clockwork soldiers in a row.
I've got better things to do
Than to waste my time on you.

II.

Robert, when I drowse to-night,
Skirting lawns of sleep to chase
Shifting dreams in mazy light,
Somewhere then I'll see your face
Turning back to bid me follow
Where I wag my arms and hollo,
Over hedges hasting after
Crooked smile and baffling laughter,
Running tireless, floating, leaping,
Down your web-hung woods and valleys,
Garden glooms and hornbeam alleys,

Where the glowworm stars are peeping,
Till I find you, quiet as stone
On a hill-top all alone,
Staring outward, gravely pondering
Jumbled leagues of hillock-wandering.

III.

You and I have walked together
In the starving winter weather.
We've been glad because we knew
Time's too short and friends are few.
We've been sad because we missed
One whose yellow head was kissed
By the gods, who thought about him
Till they couldn't do without him.
Now he's here again; I've seen
Soldier David dressed in green,
Standing in a wood that swings
To the madrigal he sings.
He's come back, all mirth and glory,
Like the prince in a fairy story.
Winter called him far away;
Blossoms bring him home with May.

IV.

Well, I know you'll swear it's true
That you found him decked in blue
Striding up through morning-land
With a cloud on either hand.
Out in Wales, you'll say, he marches
Arm-in-arm with oaks and larches;
Hides all night in hilly nooks,
Laughs at dawn in tumbling brooks.
Yet, it's certain, here he teaches
Outpost-schemes to groups of beeches.
And I'm sure, as here I stand,

That he shines through every land,
That he sings in every place
Where we're thinking of his face.

V.

Robert, there's a war in France;
Everywhere men bang and blunder,
Sweat and swear and worship Chance,
Creep and blink through cannon thunder.
Rifles crack and bullets flick,
Sing and hum like hornet-swarms.
Bones are smashed and buried quick.
Yet, through stunning battle storms,
All the while I watch the spark
Lit to guide me; for I know
Dreams will triumph, though the dark
Scowls above me where I go.
You can hear me; *you* can mingle
Radiant folly with my jingle.
War's a joke for me and you
While we know such dreams are true!

Prelude: The Troops

DIM, gradual thinning of the shapeless gloom
Shudders to drizzling daybreak that reveals
Disconsolate men who stamp their sodden boots
And turn dulled, sunken faces to the sky
Haggard and hopeless. They, who have beaten down
The stale despair of night, must now renew
Their desolation in the truce of dawn,
Murdering the livid hours that grope for peace.

Yet these, who cling to life with stubborn hands,
Can grin through storms of death and find a gap
In the clawed, cruel tangles of his defence.
They march from safety, and the bird-sung joy
Of grass-green thickets, to the land where all
Is ruin, and nothing blossoms but the sky
That hastens over them where they endure
Sad, smoking, flat horizons, reeking woods,
And foundered trench-lines volleying doom for doom.

O my brave brown companions, when your souls
Flock silently away, and the eyeless dead
Shame the wild beast of battle on the ridge,
Death will stand grieving in that field of war
Since your unvanquished hardihood is spent.
And through some mooned Valhalla there will pass
Battalions and battalions, scarred from hell;
The unreturning army that was youth;
The legions who have suffered and are dust.

Counter-Attack

WE'D gained our first objective hours before
While dawn broke like a face with blinking eyes,
Pallid, unshaved and thirsty, blind with smoke.
Things seemed all right at first. We held their line,
With bombers posted, Lewis guns well placed,
And clink of shovels deepening the shallow trench.
    The place was rotten with dead; green clumsy legs
    High-booted, sprawled and grovelled along the saps;
    And trunks, face downward, in the sucking mud,
    Wallowed like trodden sand-bags loosely filled;
    And naked sodden buttocks, mats of hair,
    Bulged, clotted heads slept in the plastering slime.
    And then the rain began,—the jolly old rain!

A yawning soldier knelt against the bank,
Staring across the morning blear with fog;
He wondered when the Allemands would get busy;
And then, of course, they started with five-nines
Traversing, sure as fate, and never a dud.
Mute in the clamour of shells he watched them burst
Spouting dark earth and wire with gusts from hell,
While posturing giants dissolved in drifts of smoke.
He crouched and flinched, dizzy with galloping fear,
Sick for escape,—loathing the strangled horror
And butchered, frantic gestures of the dead.

An officer came blundering down the trench:
"Stand-to and man the fire-step!" On he went . . .
Gasping and bawling, "Fire-step . . . counter-attack!"
    Then the haze lifted. Bombing on the right

Down the old sap: machine-guns on the left;
And stumbling figures looming out in front.
"O Christ, they're coming at us!" Bullets spat,
And he remembered his rifle . . . rapid fire . . .
And started blazing wildly . . . then a bang
Crumpled and spun him sideways, knocked him out
To grunt and wriggle: none heeded him; he choked
And fought the flapping veils of smothering gloom,
Lost in a blurred confusion of yells and groans . . .
Down, and down, and down, he sank and drowned,
Bleeding to death. The counter-attack had failed.

The Rear-Guard

(Hindenburg Line, April 1917.)

GROPING along the tunnel, step by step,
He winked his prying torch with patching glare
From side to side, and sniffed the unwholesome air.

Tins, boxes, bottles, shapes too vague to know,
A mirror smashed, the mattress from a bed;
And he, exploring fifty feet below
The rosy gloom of battle overhead.

Tripping, he grabbed the wall; saw some one lie
Humped at his feet, half-hidden by a rug,
And stooped to give the sleeper's arm a tug.
"I'm looking for headquarters." No reply.
"God blast your neck!" (For days he'd had no sleep.)
"Get up and guide me through this stinking place."
Savage, he kicked a soft, unanswering heap,
And flashed his beam across the livid face
Terribly glaring up, whose eyes yet wore
Agony dying hard ten days before;
And fists of fingers clutched a blackening wound.

Alone he staggered on until he found
Dawn's ghost that filtered down a shafted stair
To the dazed, muttering creatures underground
Who hear the boom of shells in muffled sound.
At last, with sweat of horror in his hair,
He climbed through darkness to the twilight air,
Unloading hell behind him step by step.

Wirers

"Pass it along, the wiring party's going out"—
And yawning sentries mumble, "Wirers going out."
Unravelling; twisting; hammering stakes with muffled thud,
They toil with stealthy haste and anger in their blood.

The Boche sends up a flare. Black forms stand rigid there,
Stock-still like posts; then darkness, and the clumsy ghosts
Stride hither and thither, whispering, tripped by clutching snare
Of snags and tangles.
                    Ghastly dawn with vaporous coasts
Gleams desolate along the sky, night's misery ended.

Young Hughes was badly hit; I heard him carried away,
Moaning at every lurch; no doubt he'll die to-day.
But *we* can say the front-line wire's been safely mended.

Attack

AT dawn the ridge emerges massed and dun
In the wild purple of the glowering sun,
Smouldering through spouts of drifting smoke that shroud
The menacing scarred slope; and, one by one,
Tanks creep and topple forward to the wire.
The barrage roars and lifts. Then, clumsily bowed
With bombs and guns and shovels and battle-gear,
Men jostle and climb to meet the bristling fire.
Lines of grey, muttering faces, masked with fear,
They leave their trenches, going over the top,
While time ticks blank and busy on their wrists,
And hope, with furtive eyes and grappling fists,
Flounders in mud. O Jesu, make it stop!

Dreamers

SOLDIERS are citizens of death's grey land,
    Drawing no dividend from time's to-morrows.
In the great hour of destiny they stand,
    Each with his feuds, and jealousies, and sorrows.
Soldiers are sworn to action; they must win
    Some flaming, fatal climax with their lives.
Soldiers are dreamers; when the guns begin
    They think of firelit homes, clean beds, and wives.

I see them in foul dug-outs, gnawed by rats,
    And in the ruined trenches, lashed with rain,
Dreaming of things they did with balls and bats,
    And mocked by hopeless longing to regain
Bank-holidays, and picture shows, and spats,
    And going to the office in the train.

How to Die

DARK clouds are smouldering into red
    While down the craters morning burns.
The dying soldier shifts his head
    To watch the glory that returns:
He lifts his fingers toward the skies
    Where holy brightness breaks in flame;
Radiance reflected in his eyes,
    And on his lips a whispered name.

You'd think, to hear some people talk,
    That lads go West with sobs and curses,
And sullen faces white as chalk,
    Hankering for wreaths and tombs and hearses.
But they've been taught the way to do it
    Like Christian soldiers; not with haste
And shuddering groans; but passing through it
    With due regard for decent taste.

The Effect

> "The effect of our bombardment was terrific. One man
> told me he had never seen so many dead before."
> —*War Correspondent.*

"He'd never seen so many dead before."
They sprawled in yellow daylight while he swore
And gasped and lugged his everlasting load
Of bombs along what once had been a road.
"How peaceful are the dead."
Who put that silly gag in some one's head?

"He'd never seen so many dead before."
The lilting words danced up and down his brain,
While corpses jumped and capered in the rain.
No, no; he wouldn't count them any more . . .
The dead have done with pain:
They've choked; they can't come back to life again.

When Dick was killed last week he looked like that,
Flapping along the fire-step like a fish,
After the blazing crump had knocked him flat . . .
*"How many dead? As many as ever you wish.
Don't count 'em; they're too many.
Who'll buy my nice fresh corpses, two a penny?"*

Twelve Months After

HULLO! here's my platoon, the lot I had last year.
"The war'll be over soon."
                              "What 'opes?"
                                              "No bloody fear!"
Then, "Number Seven, 'shun! All present and correct."
They're standing in the sun, impassive and erect.
Young Gibson with his grin; and Morgan, tired and white;
Jordan, who's out to win a D.C.M. some night;
And Hughes that's keen on wiring; and Davies ('79),
Who always must be firing at the Boche front line.

                  ✿   ✿   ✿   ✿   ✿

"Old soldiers never die; they simply fide a-why!"
That's what they used to sing along the roads last spring;
That's what they used to say before the push began;
That's where they are to-day, knocked over to a man.

The Fathers

SNUG at the club two fathers sat,
Gross, goggle-eyed, and full of chat.
One of them said: "My eldest lad
Writes cheery letters from Bagdad.
But Arthur's getting all the fun
At Arras with his nine-inch gun."

"Yes," wheezed the other, "that's the luck!
My boy's quite broken-hearted, stuck
In England training all this year.
Still, if there's truth in what we hear,
The Huns intend to ask for more
    Before they bolt across the Rhine."
I watched them toddle through the door—
    These impotent old friends of mine.

Base Details

IF I were fierce, and bald, and short of breath,
    I'd live with scarlet Majors at the Base,
And speed glum heroes up the line to death.
    You'd see me with my puffy petulant face,
Guzzling and gulping in the best hotel,
    Reading the Roll of Honour. "Poor young chap,"
I'd say—"I used to know his father well;
    Yes, we've lost heavily in this last scrap."
And when the war is done and youth stone dead,
I'd toddle safely home and die—in bed.

The General

"GOOD-MORNING; good-morning!" the General said
When we met him last week on our way to the line.
Now the soldiers he smiled at are most of 'em dead,
And we're cursing his staff for incompetent swine.
"He's a cheery old card," grunted Harry to Jack
As they slogged up to Arras with rifle and pack.

    ✿   ✿   ✿   ✿   ✿

But he did for them both by his plan of attack.

Lamentations

I FOUND him in the guard-room at the Base.
From the blind darkness I had heard his crying
And blundered in. With puzzled, patient face
A sergeant watched him; it was no good trying
To stop it; for he howled and beat his chest.
And, all because his brother had gone West,
Raved at the bleeding war; his rampant grief
Moaned, shouted, sobbed, and choked, while he was kneeling
Half-naked on the floor. In my belief
Such men have lost all patriotic feeling.

Does It Matter?

Does it matter?—losing your leg? . . .
For people will always be kind,
And you need not show that you mind
When the others come in after hunting
To gobble their muffins and eggs.

Does it matter?—losing your sight? . . .
There's such splendid work for the blind;
And people will always be kind,
As you sit on the terrace remembering
And turning your face to the light.

Do they matter?—those dreams from the pit? . . .
You can drink and forget and be glad,
And people won't say that you're mad;
For they'll know that you've fought for your country,
And no one will worry a bit.

Fight to a Finish

THE boys came back. Bands played and flags were flying,
　　And Yellow-Pressmen thronged the sunlit street
To cheer the soldiers who'd refrained from dying,
　　And hear the music of returning feet.
"Of all the thrills and ardours War has brought,
This moment is the finest." (So they thought.)

Snapping their bayonets on to charge the mob,
　　Grim Fusiliers broke ranks with glint of steel.
At last the boys had found a cushy job.
　　　　❖　❖　❖　❖　❖
　　I heard the Yellow-Pressmen grunt and squeal;
And with my trusty bombers turned and went
To clear those Junkers out of Parliament.

Editorial Impressions

HE seemed so certain "all was going well,"
As he discussed the glorious time he'd had
While visiting the trenches.
                              "One can tell
You've gathered big impressions!" grinned the lad
Who'd been severely wounded in the back
In some wiped-out impossible Attack.
"Impressions? Yes, most vivid! I am writing
A little book called *Europe on the Rack*,
Based on notes made while witnessing the fighting.
I hope I've caught the feeling of 'the Line,'
And the amazing spirit of the troops.
By Jove, those flying-chaps of ours are fine!
I watched one daring beggar looping loops,
Soaring and diving like some bird of prey.
And through it all I felt that splendour shine
Which makes us win."
                              The soldier sipped his wine.
"Ah, yes, but it's the Press that leads the way!"

Suicide in the Trenches

I KNEW a simple soldier boy
Who grinned at life in empty joy,
Slept soundly through the lonesome dark,
And whistled early with the lark.

In winter trenches, cowed and glum,
With crumps and lice and lack of rum,
He put a bullet through his brain.
No one spoke of him again.

    ✶   ✶   ✶   ✶   ✶

You snug-faced crowds with kindling eye
Who cheer when soldier lads march by,
Sneak home and pray you'll never know
The hell where youth and laughter go.

Glory of Women

YOU love us when we're heroes, home on leave,
Or wounded in a mentionable place.
You worship decorations; you believe
That chivalry redeems the war's disgrace.
You make us shells. You listen with delight,
By tales of dirt and danger fondly thrilled.
You crown our distant ardours while we fight,
And mourn our laurelled memories when we're killed.

You can't believe that British troops "retire"
When hell's last horror breaks them, and they run,
Trampling the terrible corpses—blind with blood.
　　O German mother dreaming by the fire,
　　While you are knitting socks to send your son
　　His face is trodden deeper in the mud.

Their Frailty

HE's got a Blighty wound. He's safe; and then
　　War's fine and bold and bright.
She can forget the doomed and prisoned men
　　Who agonize and fight.

He's back in France. She loathes the listless strain
　　And peril of his plight.
Beseeching Heaven to send him home again,
　　She prays for peace each night.

Husbands and sons and lovers; everywhere
　　They die; War bleeds us white.
Mothers and wives and sweethearts,—they don't care
　　So long as He's all right.

The Hawthorn Tree

Not much to me is yonder lane
  Where I go every day;
But when there's been a shower of rain
  And hedge-birds whistle gay,
I know my lad that's out in France
  With fearsome things to see
Would give his eyes for just one glance
  At our white hawthorn tree.

  ✿   ✿   ✿   ✿   ✿

Not much to me is yonder lane
  Where *he* so longs to tread;
But when there's been a shower of rain
I think I'll never weep again
  Until I've heard he's dead.

The Investiture

GOD with a Roll of Honour in His hand
Sits welcoming the heroes who have died,
While sorrowless angels ranked on either side
Stand easy in Elysium's meadow-land.
Then *you* come shyly through the garden gate,
Wearing a blood-soaked bandage on your head;
And God says something kind because you're dead,
And homesick, discontented with your fate.

If I were there we'd snowball Death with skulls;
Or ride away to hunt in Devil's Wood
With ghosts of puppies that we walked of old.
But you're alone; and solitude annuls
Our earthly jokes; and strangely wise and good
You roam forlorn along the streets of gold.

Trench Duty

SHAKEN from sleep, and numbed and scarce awake,
Out in the trench with three hours' watch to take,
I blunder through the splashing mirk; and then
Hear the gruff muttering voices of the men
Crouching in cabins candle-chinked with light.
Hark! There's the big bombardment on our right
Rumbling and bumping; and the dark's a glare
Of flickering horror in the sectors where
We raid the Boche; men waiting, stiff and chilled,
Or crawling on their bellies through the wire.
"What? Stretcher-bearers wanted? Some one killed?"
Five minutes ago I heard a sniper fire:
Why did he do it? . . . Starlight overhead—
Blank stars. I'm wide-awake; and some chap's dead.

Break of Day

THERE seemed a smell of autumn in the air
At the bleak end of night; he shivered there
In a dank, musty dug-out where he lay,
Legs wrapped in sand-bags,—lumps of chalk and clay
Spattering his face. Dry-mouthed, he thought, "To-day
We start the damned attack; and, Lord knows why,
Zero's at nine; how bloody if I'm done in
Under the freedom of that morning sky!"
And then he coughed and dozed, cursing the din.

Was it the ghost of autumn in that smell
Of underground, or God's blank heart grown kind,
That sent a happy dream to him in hell?—
Where men are crushed like clods, and crawl to find
Some crater for their wretchedness; who lie
In outcast immolation, doomed to die
Far from clean things or any hope of cheer,
Cowed anger in their eyes, till darkness brims
And roars into their heads, and they can hear
Old childish talk, and tags of foolish hymns.

He sniffs the chilly air; (his dreaming starts).
He's riding in a dusty Sussex lane
In quiet September; slowly night departs;
And he's a living soul, absolved from pain.
Beyond the brambled fences where he goes
Are glimmering fields with harvest piled in sheaves,
And tree-tops dark against the stars grown pale;
Then, clear and shrill, a distant farm-cock crows;
And there's a wall of mist along the vale

Where willows shake their watery-sounding leaves.
He gazes on it all, and scarce believes
That earth is telling its old peaceful tale;
He thanks the blessed world that he was born . . .
Then, far away, a lonely note of the horn.

They're drawing the Big Wood! Unlatch the gate,
And set Golumpus going on the grass:
He knows the corner where it's best to wait
And hear the crashing woodland chorus pass;
The corner where old foxes make their track
To the Long Spinney; that's the place to be.
The bracken shakes below an ivied tree,
And then a cub looks out; and "Tally-o-back!"
He bawls, and swings his thong with volleying crack,—
All the clean thrill of autumn in his blood,
And hunting surging through him like a flood
In joyous welcome from the untroubled past;
While the war drifts away, forgotten at last.

Now a red, sleepy sun above the rim
Of twilight stares along the quiet weald,
And the kind, simple country shines revealed
In solitudes of peace, no longer dim.
The old horse lifts his face and thanks the light,
Then stretches down his head to crop the green.
All things that he has loved are in his sight;
The places where his happiness has been
Are in his eyes, his heart, and they are good.

       ❖   ❖   ❖   ❖   ❖

Hark! there's the horn: they're drawing the Big Wood.

To Any Dead Officer

WELL, how are things in Heaven? I wish you'd say,
  Because I'd like to know that you're all right.
Tell me, have you found everlasting day,
  Or been sucked in by everlasting night?
For when I shut my eyes your face shows pain;
  I hear you make some cheery old remark—
I can rebuild you in my brain,
  Though you've gone out patrolling in the dark.

You hated tours of trenches; you were proud
  Of nothing more than having good years to spend;
Longed to get home and join the careless crowd
  Of chaps who work in peace with Time for friend.
That's all washed out now. You're beyond the wire:
  No earthly chance can send you crawling back;
You've finished with machine-gun fire—
  Knocked over in a hopeless dud-attack.

Somehow I always thought you'd get done in,
  Because you were so desperate keen to live:
You were all out to try and save your skin,
  Well knowing how much the world had got to give.
You joked at shells and talked the usual "shop,"
  Stuck to your dirty job and did it fine:
With "Jesus Christ! when *will* it stop?
  Three years. . . . It's hell unless we break their line."

So when they told me you'd been left for dead
  I wouldn't believe them, feeling it *must* be true.
Next week the bloody Roll of Honour said

"Wounded and missing"—(That's the thing to do
When lads are left in shell-holes dying slow,
    With nothing but blank sky and wounds that ache,
Moaning for water till they know
    It's night, and then it's not worth while to wake!)

       ✿   ✿   ✿   ✿   ✿

Good-bye, old lad! Remember me to God,
    And tell Him that our Politicians swear
They won't give in till Prussian Rule's been trod
    Under the Heel of England. . . . Are you there? . . .
Yes . . . and the War won't end for at least two years;
But we've got stacks of men. . . . I'm blind with tears,
    Staring into the dark. Cheero!
I wish they'd killed you in a decent show.

Sick Leave

WHEN I'm asleep, dreaming and lulled and warm,—
They come, the homeless ones, the noiseless dead.
While the dim charging breakers of the storm
Bellow and drone and rumble overhead,
Out of the gloom they gather about my bed.
  They whisper to my heart; their thoughts are mine.
  "Why are you here with all your watches ended?
  From Ypres to Frise we sought you in the Line."
In bitter safety I awake, unfriended;
And while the dawn begins with slashing rain
I think of the Battalion in the mud.
"When are you going out to them again?
Are they not still your brothers through our blood?"

Banishment

I AM banished from the patient men who fight.
They smote my heart to pity, built my pride.
Shoulder to aching shoulder, side by side,
They trudged away from life's broad wealds of light.
Their wrongs were mine; and ever in my sight
They went arrayed in honour. But they died,—
Not one by one: and mutinous I cried
To those who sent them out into the night.

The darkness tells how vainly I have striven
To free them from the pit where they must dwell
In outcast gloom convulsed and jagged and riven
By grappling guns. Love drove me to rebel.
Love drives me back to grope with them through hell;
And in their tortured eyes I stand forgiven.

Song-Books of the War

In fifty years, when peace outshines
Remembrance of the battle lines,
Adventurous lads will sigh and cast
Proud looks upon the plundered past.
On summer morn or winter's night,
Their hearts will kindle for the fight,
Reading a snatch of soldier-song,
Savage and jaunty, fierce and strong;
And through the angry marching rhymes
Of blind regret and haggard mirth,
They'll envy us the dazzling times
When sacrifice absolved our earth.

Some ancient man with silver locks
Will lift his weary face to say:
"War was a fiend who stopped our clocks
Although we met him grim and gay."
And then he'll speak of Haig's last drive,
Marvelling that any came alive
Out of the shambles that men built
And smashed, to cleanse the world of guilt.
But the boys, with grin and sidelong glance,
Will think, "Poor grandad's day is done."
And dream of those who fought in France
And lived in time to share the fun.

Thrushes

TOSSED on the glittering air they soar and skim,
Whose voices make the emptiness of light
A windy palace. Quavering from the brim
Of dawn, and bold with song at edge of night,
They clutch their leafy pinnacles and sing
Scornful of man, and from his toils aloof
Whose heart's a haunted woodland whispering;
Whose thoughts return on tempest-baffled wing;
Who hears the cry of God in everything,
And storms the gate of nothingness for proof.

Autumn

OCTOBER'S bellowing anger breaks and cleaves
The bronzed battalions of the stricken wood
In whose lament I hear a voice that grieves
For battle's fruitless harvest, and the feud
Of outraged men. Their lives are like the leaves
Scattered in flocks of ruin, tossed and blown
Along the westering furnace flaring red.
O martyred youth and manhood overthrown,
The burden of your wrongs is on my head.

Invocation

COME down from heaven to meet me when my breath
Chokes, and through drumming shafts of stifling death
I stumble toward escape, to find the door
Opening on morn where I may breathe once more
Clear cock-crow airs across some valley dim
With whispering trees. While dawn along the rim
Of night's horizon flows in lakes of fire,
Come down from heaven's bright hill, my song's desire.

Belov'd and faithful, teach my soul to wake
In glades deep-ranked with flowers that gleam and shake
And flock your paths with wonder. In your gaze
Show me the vanquished vigil of my days.
Mute in that golden silence hung with green,
Come down from heaven and bring me in your eyes
Remembrance of all beauty that has been,
And stillness from the pools of Paradise.

Repression of War Experience

Now light the candles; one; two; there's a moth;
What silly beggars they are to blunder in
And scorch their wings with glory, liquid flame—
No, no, not that,—it's bad to think of war,
When thoughts you've gagged all day come back to scare you;
And it's been proved that soldiers don't go mad
Unless they lose control of ugly thoughts
That drive them out to jabber among the trees.

   Now light your pipe; look, what a steady hand,
Draw a deep breath; stop thinking, count fifteen,
And you're as right as rain. . . .
                  Why won't it rain? . . .
I wish there'd be a thunder-storm to-night,
With bucketsful of water to sluice the dark,
And make the roses hang their dripping heads.

Books; what a jolly company they are,
Standing so quiet and patient on their shelves,
Dressed in dim brown, and black, and white, and green,
And every kind of colour. Which will you read?
Come on; O *do* read something; they're so wise.
I tell you all the wisdom of the world
Is waiting for you on those shelves; and yet
You sit and gnaw your nails, and let your pipe out,
And listen to the silence: on the ceiling
There's one big, dizzy moth that bumps and flutters;
And in the breathless air outside the house
The garden waits for something that delays.
There must be crowds of ghosts among the trees,—

Not people killed in battle,—they're in France,—
But horrible shapes in shrouds—old men who died
Slow, natural deaths,—old men with ugly souls,
Who wore their bodies out with nasty sins.

     ✿   ✿   ✿   ✿   ✿

You're quiet and peaceful, summering safe at home;
You'd never think there was a bloody war on! . . .
O yes, you would . . . why, you can hear the guns.
Hark! Thud, thud, thud,—quite soft . . . they never cease—
Those whispering guns—O Christ, I want to go out
And screech at them to stop—I'm going crazy;
I'm going stark, staring mad because of the guns.

The Triumph

WHEN life was a cobweb of stars for Beauty who came
  In the whisper of leaves or a bird's lone cry in the glen,
On dawn-lit hills and horizons girdled with flame
  I sought for the triumph that troubles the faces of men.

With death in the terrible flickering gloom of the fight
  I was cruel and fierce with despair; I was naked and bound;
I was stricken: and Beauty returned through the shambles of
    night;
  In the faces of men she returned; and their triumph I found.

Survivors

No doubt they'll soon get well; the shock and strain
    Have caused their stammering, disconnected talk.
Of course they're "longing to go out again,"—
    These boys with old, scared faces, learning to walk,
They'll soon forget their haunted nights; their cowed
    Subjection to the ghosts of friends who died,—
Their dreams that drip with murder; and they'll be proud
    Of glorious war that shatter'd all their pride . . .
Men who went out to battle, grim and glad;
Children, with eyes that hate you, broken and mad.

CRAIGLOCKHART,
    Oct. 1917.

Joy-Bells

RING your sweet bells; but let them be farewells
  To the green-vista'd gladness of the past
That changed us into soldiers; swing your bells
  To a joyful chime; but let it be the last.

What means this metal in windy belfries hung
  When guns are all our need? Dissolve these bells
Whose tones are tuned for peace: with martial tongue
  Let them cry doom and storm the sun with shells.

Bells are like fierce-browed prelates who proclaim
  That "if our Lord returned He'd fight for *us*."
So let our bells and bishops do the same,
  Shoulder to shoulder with the motor bus.

Remorse

Lost in the swamp and welter of the pit,
He flounders off the duck-boards; only he knows
Each flash and spouting crash,—each instant lit
When gloom reveals the streaming rain. He goes
Heavily, blindly on. And, while he blunders,
"Could anything be worse than this!"—he wonders,
Remembering how he saw those Germans run,
Screaming for mercy among the stumps of trees:
Green-faced, they dodged and darted: there was one
Livid with terror, clutching at his knees. . . .
Our chaps were sticking 'em like pigs. . . . "O hell!"
He thought—"there's things in war one dare not tell
Poor father sitting safe at home, who reads
Of dying heroes and their deathless deeds."

Dead Musicians

I.

FROM you, Beethoven, Bach, Mozart,
   The substance of my dreams took fire.
You built cathedrals in my heart,
   And lit my pinnacled desire.
You were the ardour and the bright
   Procession of my thoughts toward prayer.
You were the wrath of storm, the light
   On distant citadels aflare.

II.

Great names, I cannot find you now
   In these loud years of youth that strives
Through doom toward peace: upon my brow
   I wear a wreath of banished lives.
You have no part with lads who fought
   And laughed and suffered at my side.
Your fugues and symphonies have brought
   No memory of my friends who died.

III.

For when my brain is on their track,
In slangy speech I call them back.
With fox-trot tunes their ghosts I charm.
"Another little drink won't do us any harm."
   I think of rag-time; a bit of rag-time;
   And see their faces crowding round

To the sound of the syncopated beat.
They've got such jolly things to tell,
Home from hell with a Blighty wound so neat. . . .

      ❀   ❀   ❀   ❀   ❀

And so the song breaks off; and I'm alone.
They're dead. . . . For God's sake stop that gramophone.

The Dream

I.

MOONLIGHT and dew-drenched blossom, and the scent
Of summer gardens; these can bring you all
Those dreams that in the starlit silence fall:
Sweet songs are full of odours.
                              While I went
Last night in drizzling dusk along a lane,
I passed a squalid farm; from byre and midden
Came the rank smell that brought me once again
A dream of war that in the past was hidden.

II.

Up a disconsolate straggling village street
I saw the tired troops trudge: I heard their feet.
The cheery Q.M.S. was there to meet
And guide our Company in . . .
                         I watched them stumble
Into some crazy hovel, too beat to grumble;
Saw them file inward, slipping from their backs
Rifles, equipment, packs.
On filthy straw they sit in the gloom, each face
Bowed to patched, sodden boots they must unlace,
While the wind chills their sweat through chinks and cracks.

III.

I'm looking at their blistered feet; young Jones
Stares up at me, mud-splashed and white and jaded;

Out of his eyes the morning light has faded.
Old soldiers with three winters in their bones
Puff their damp Woodbines, whistle, stretch their toes:
They can still grin at me, for each of 'em knows
That I'm as tired as they are . . .

                    Can they guess
The secret burden that is always mine?—
Pride in their courage; pity for their distress;
And burning bitterness
That I must take them to the accursèd Line.

IV.

I cannot hear their voices, but I see
Dim candles in the barn: they gulp their tea,
And soon they'll sleep like logs. Ten miles away
The battle winks and thuds in blundering strife.
And I must lead them nearer, day by day,
To the foul beast of war that bludgeons life.

In Barracks

THE barrack-square, washed clean with rain,
Shines wet and wintry-grey and cold.
Young Fusiliers, strong-legged and bold,
March and wheel and march again.
The sun looks over the barrack gate,
Warm and white with glaring shine,
To watch the soldiers of the Line
That life has hired to fight with fate.

Fall out: the long parades are done.
Up comes the dark; down goes the sun.
The square is walled with windowed light.
Sleep well, you lusty Fusiliers;
Shut your brave eyes on sense and sight,
And banish from your dreamless ears
The bugle's lying notes that say,
"Another night; another day."

Together

SPLASHING along the boggy woods all day,
And over brambled hedge and holding clay,
I shall not think of him:
But when the watery fields grow brown and dim,
And hounds have lost their fox, and horses tire,
I know that he'll be with me on my way
Home through the darkness to the evening fire.

He's jumped each stile along the glistening lanes;
His hand will be upon the mud-soaked reins;
Hearing the saddle creak,
He'll wonder if the frost will come next week.
I shall forget him in the morning light;
And while we gallop on he will not speak:
But at the stable-door he'll say good-night.

Battalion Relief

"Fall in! Now get a move on!" (Curse the rain.)
We splash away along the straggling village,
Out to the flat rich country, green with June . . .
And sunset flares across wet crops and tillage,
Blazing with splendour-patches. Harvest soon
Up in the Line. *"Perhaps the War'll be done
By Christmas-time. Keep smiling then, old son!"*

Here's the Canal: it's dusk; we cross the bridge.
"Lead on there by platoons." The Line's a-glare
With shell-fire through the poplars; distant rattle
Of rifles and machine-guns. *"Fritz is there!
Christ, ain't it lively, Sergeant? Is't a battle?"*
More rain: the lightning blinks, and thunder rumbles.
"There's overhead artillery!" some chap grumbles.

"What's all this mob, by the cross-road?" (The guides) . . .
"Lead on with Number One." (And off they go.)
"Three-minute intervals." . . . Poor blundering files,
Sweating and blindly burdened; who's to know
If death will catch them in those two dark miles?
(More rain.) *"Lead on, Headquarters."* (That's the lot.)
*"Who's that? O, Sergeant-major; don't get shot!
And tell me, have we won this war or not?"*

The Dug-Out

WHY do you lie with your legs ungainly huddled,
And one arm bent across your sullen cold
Exhausted face? It hurts my heart to watch you,
Deep-shadow'd from the candle's guttering gold;
And you wonder why I shake you by the shoulder;
Drowsy, you mumble and sigh and turn your head . . .
You are too young to fall asleep for ever;
And when you sleep you remind me of the dead.

I Stood With the Dead

I STOOD with the Dead, so forsaken and still:
  When dawn was grey I stood with the Dead.
And my slow heart said, "You must kill, you must kill:
  Soldier, soldier, morning is red."

On the shapes of the slain in their crumpled disgrace
  I stared for a while through the thin cold rain. . . .
"O lad that I loved, there is rain on your face,
  And your eyes are blurred and sick like the plain."

I stood with the Dead. . . . They were dead; they were dead;
  My heart and my head beat a march of dismay:
And gusts of the wind came dulled by the guns . . .
  "Fall in!" I shouted; "Fall in for your pay!"

In an Underground Dressing-Station

QUIETLY they set their burden down: he tried
To grin; moaned; moved his head from side to side.

         ✿   ✿   ✿   ✿   ✿

He gripped the stretcher; stiffened; glared; and screamed,
"O put my leg down, doctor, do!" (He'd got
A bullet in his ankle; and he'd been shot
Horribly through the guts.) The surgeon seemed
So kind and gentle, saying, above that crying,
"You *must* keep still, my lad." But he was dying.

Atrocities

You told me, in your drunken-boasting mood,
How once you butchered prisoners. That was good!
I'm sure you felt no pity while they stood
Patient and cowed and scared, as prisoners should.

How did you do them in? Come, don't be shy:
You know I love to hear how Germans die,
Downstairs in dug-outs. "Camerad!" they cry;
Then squeal like stoats when bombs begin to fly.

      ✦   ✦   ✦   ✦   ✦

And you? I know your record. You went sick
When orders looked unwholesome: then, with trick
And lie, you wangled home. And here you are,
Still talking big and boozing in a bar.

Return of the Heroes

A lady watches from the crowd,
Enthusiastic, flushed, and proud.

"OH! there's Sir Henry Dudster! Such a splendid leader!
How pleased he looks! What rows of ribbons on his tunic!
Such dignity . . . Saluting . . . *(Wave your flag . . . now, Freda!)* . . .
Yes, dear, I saw a Prussian General once,—at Munich.

"Here's the next carriage! . . . Jack was once in Leggit's Corps;
That's him! . . . I think the stout one is Sir Godfrey Stoomer.
They *must* feel sad to know they can't win any more
Great victories! . . . Aren't they glorious men? . . . so full of
    humour!"

Concert Party

THEY are gathering round . . .
Out of the twilight; over the grey-blue sand,
Shoals of low-jargoning men drift inward to the sound,—
The jangle and throb of a piano . . . tum-ti-tum . . .
Drawn by a lamp, they come
Out of the glimmering lines of their tents, over the shuffling
    sand.

O sing us the songs, the songs of our own land,
You warbling ladies in white.
Dimness conceals the hunger in our faces,
This wall of faces risen out of the night,
These eyes that keep their memories of the places
So long beyond their sight.

Jaded and gay, the ladies sing; and the chap in brown
Tilts his grey hat; jaunty and lean and pale,
He rattles the keys . . . some actor-bloke from town . . .
"God send you home"; and then "A long, long trail";
"I hear you calling me"; and "Dixieland" . . .
Sing slowly . . . now the chorus . . . one by one
We hear them, drink them; till the concert's done.
Silent, I watch the shadowy mass of soldiers stand.
Silent, they drift away, over the glimmering sand.

KANTARA,
    April, 1918.

Night on the Convoy

[ALEXANDRIA–MARSEILLES]

OUT in the blustering darkness, on the deck
A gleam of stars looks down. Long blurs of black,
The lean Destroyers, level with our track,
Plunging and stealing, watch the perilous way
Through backward racing seas and caverns of chill spray.

One sentry by the davits, in the gloom
Stands mute: the boat heaves onward through the night.
Shrouded is every chink of cabined light:
And sluiced by floundering waves that hiss and boom
And crash like guns, the troop-ship shudders . . . doom.

Now something at my feet stirs with a sigh;
And slowly growing used to groping dark,
I know that the hurricane-deck, down all its length,
Is heaped and spread with lads in sprawling strength,—
Blanketed soldiers sleeping. In the stark
Danger of life at war, they lie so still,
All prostrate and defenceless, head by head . . .
And I remember Arras, and that hill
Where dumb with pain I stumbled among the dead.

✿   ✿   ✿   ✿   ✿

We are going home. The troop-ship, in a thrill
Of fiery-chamber'd anguish, throbs and rolls.
We are going home . . . victims . . . three thousand souls.

May, 1918.

Reconciliation

WHEN you are standing at your hero's grave,
Or near some homeless village where he died,
Remember, through your heart's rekindling pride,
The German soldiers who were loyal and brave.

Men fought like brutes; and hideous things were done;
And you have nourished hatred, harsh and blind.
But in that Golgotha perhaps you'll find
The mothers of the men who killed your son.

November, 1918.

Memorial Tablet

[GREAT WAR]

SQUIRE nagged and bullied till I went to fight
(Under Lord Derby's scheme). I died in hell—
(They called it Passchendaele); my wound was slight,
And I was hobbling back, and then a shell
Burst slick upon the duck-boards; so I fell
Into the bottomless mud, and lost the light.

In sermon-time, while Squire is in his pew,
He gives my gilded name a thoughtful stare;
For though low down upon the list, I'm there:
"In proud and glorious memory"—that's my due.
Two bleeding years I fought in France for Squire;
I suffered anguish that he's never guessed;
Once I came home on leave; and then went west.
What greater glory could a man desire?

Aftermath

Have you forgotten yet? . . .
For the world's events have rumbled on since those gagged days,
Like traffic checked awhile at the crossing of city ways:
And the haunted gap in your mind has filled with thoughts that
  flow
Like clouds in the lit heavens of life; and you're a man reprieved
  to go,
Taking your peaceful share of Time, with joy to spare.
But the past is just the same,—and War's a bloody game. . . .
Have you forgotten yet? . . .
*Look down, and swear by the slain of the War that you'll never
  forget.*

Do you remember the dark months you held the sector at
  Mametz,—
The nights you watched and wired and dug and piled sandbags
  on parapets?
Do you remember the rats; and the stench
Of corpses rotting in front of the front-line trench,—
And dawn coming, dirty-white, and chill with a hopeless rain?
Do you ever stop and ask, "Is it all going to happen again?"

Do you remember that hour of din before the attack,—
And the anger, the blind compassion that seized and shook you
  then
As you peered at the doomed and haggard faces of your men?
Do you remember the stretcher-cases lurching back
With dying eyes and lolling heads,—those ashen-grey
Masks of the lads who once were keen and kind and gay?

Have you forgotten yet? . . .
Look up, and swear by the green of the Spring that you'll never
forget.

Everyone Sang

EVERYONE suddenly burst out singing;
And I was filled with such delight
As prisoned birds must find in freedom
Winging wildly across the white
Orchards and dark green fields; on; on; and out of sight.

Everyone's voice was suddenly lifted,
And beauty came like the setting sun.
My heart was shaken with tears and horror
Drifted away . . . O but every one
Was a bird; and the song was wordless; the singing will never be
    done.

April, 1919.

Memory

WHEN I was young my heart and head were light,
And I was gay and feckless as a colt
Out in the fields, with morning in the may,
Wind on the grass, wings in the orchard bloom.
    O thrilling sweet, my joy, when life was free,
    And all the paths led on from hawthorn-time
    Across the carolling meadows into June.

But now my heart is heavy-laden. I sit
Burning my dreams away beside the fire:
For death has made me wise and bitter and strong;
And I am rich in all that I have lost.
    O starshine on the fields of long-ago,
    Bring me the darkness and the nightingale;
    Dim wealds of vanished summer, peace of home,
    And silence; and the faces of my friends.

Devotion to Duty

I WAS near the King that day. I saw him snatch
And briskly scan the G.H.Q. dispatch.
Thick-voiced, he read it out. (His face was grave.)
"This officer advanced with the first wave,
"And when our first objective had been gained,
"(Though wounded twice), reorganized the line:
"The spirit of the troops was by his fine
"Example most effectively sustained."

He gripped his beard; then closed his eyes and said,
"Bathsheba must be warned that he is dead.
"Send for her. I will be the first to tell
"This wife how her heroic husband fell."

Alphabetical Index of Titles

Alphabetical Index of First Lines